Surviving motherhood through self love..

jasmin Johnson

BookLeaf
Publishing

Presentation by *BookLeaf Publishing*

Web: www.bookleafpub.com

E-mail: info@bookleafpub.com

ISBN: 9789357697224

First edition 2023

DEDICATION

This book is dedicated to those who are living in hope

To those going in and out of anxiety phases

To those striving to hold on to motivation but it slips away

To those trying to find a way to hold on to it

To those who are searching for a feeling in order to believe, manifest, and create a life where you no longer have to fight for what is right

For those battling with self identity and a sense of belonging

For those that think that these little affirmations are tedious as fuck! that at times it gets so discouraging

I dedicate this book to my bonus daughter Samaira who has been witnessing this journey with me while I was trying to digest these affirmations in the morning to make it easier to raise her at times.

To realizing how much shifting my thoughts could make an experience so much smoother

ACKNOWLEDGEMENT

I like to acknowledge my partner for believing in me, seeing the highest potential that I didn't see in my self. Thank you for your patience, your real ass nigga energy! lol!! love and support I love you King! Thanks to my best friend for always reminding me of the depths on why I am here in the first place, reminding me of what I will deal with if I don't do what I am called to do here. Thanks to my daughter Amunet for coming into this world and giving me the words to write.

Her existence allows me to reflect on life before her, which I don't know what it would've been like with her being so special to me. thanks to Samaira for the amount of strength you have helped me gain through mothership with you before having my very own, also bringing the inner child out of me every time continue to shine bright I love you!

PREFACE

" When people tell you affirmations don't work, don't believe them!"
                              "believe in yourself"

I have daddy issues

I have daddy issues
because I went from feeling that pure love
and excitement when it was about seeing you
to going in my room and closing the door as
soon as I hear you
how did you develop the urge to have sexual
thoughts and feelings about me
hey watching porn wasn't the best for me at
the time
but instead you got aroused at the fact that I was
on my way to being ahead of my time
but you didn't stop me because glady
the dick in your pants
continued to get happy
but I continued to enter the room
when you asked me
because you kept begging me to stay
instead of begging my motha to play
yea she played a role
and you wasn't one of them
so you found a way to control
the gullible one
got me listening to the reasons
why teaching me that teasing
would fulfill your reason
that touching and licking me was okay

because we aren't blood anyways
and so its okay
it won't affect you
as long you dont tell nobody
we good
hey
I love you
though I grew up super weird about men
I enjoyed myself with women too
I knew that I could fuck men
and not even catch feelings whew!
its what I learned
from that situation back then
here I am
sometimes I question what I feel
knowing that there's a story that plays in my
head that is real
I put a lot of pressure in trying to be myself
but how can I walk around
like I'm good knowing that
there's a truth
laying in my own roof
as much as I tried to bury
but at times when its time to release
that sexual energy
those thoughts arises
where I realize
I didn't bury it deep enough
so the universe is saying

my dear you have to write a rough
one time I started but I draft it quick as fuck
here I am again I think I wrote enough..

Dear mothers

please be mindful of your daughters
when you aren't fucking their ill fathers
as they are trying to stay loyal by you
so instead they go after their daughters
remember something mothers
just like you notice their bodies changing so
does their fathers
but their not saying shit
because its uncomfortable to see the fact that
their daughters are growing bodies
and looking like the girls
in the streets that they bodied
I know this is very uncomfortable
but please I am here to remind you to be mindful
hey
fathers
dont stick around if you feel you are in need
go on and cheat if you have to
leave your daughters alone
that you think you own
because you invested your time and energy on
them
until they've grown..

I am enough

I am enough
Is what I tell myself
Over and over again
Because back then
When my mama asked
Me to do something
It was never good enough
She would do it over in front of me
Over and over again
complaining
That i didn't do it just like her
But
I was a kid with less experiences then her
But that wasn't the perspective for her
To her it was like how don't you get this?
It was like Your supposed to do it until you see
nothing
Nothing? Does that really exist?
Because to me there is always something
And doing nothing is really a struggle for me
now
So i struggle with always doing something
Because if I do nothing
I don't feel worthy
Enough

Like taking a thousand pictures with the same
outfit
And still
is not enough
So yea fuck a filter
Once upon a time I enjoyed real picturess
How did we become so obsessive with
perfection?
Yesterday I had a conversation with my best
friend
I told her that this is one of my struggles
And I am ready to embrace it
I asked my oldest the other day
Do I ever make her feel like she have to be
perfect?
She said yea
I said I am sorry
She said its okay, I know how to deal with it
I said how do you deal with it?
She said I don't let it get to me because I know
perfection will never be
And I know you deal with some things from
your childhood
So sometimes you just take it out on me
But it ain't me
All I could do is hug her and kiss her
Tell her I love her…

Hiding is real

Hiding is real
Because there's so much shit mistaken these
days as big deals
I'm a real dork at heart
Admitting that to you all
be may the hardest part
Matter fact I'm not hiding no more
I love me to the core
I been around a lot people
Who don't love themselves enough
Thought something was wrong with me
For Loving myself enough
So I back down
Just so I can have some type of fun
Because being real
Felt like constantly being on the run
Instead I was running
Running from myself
Because I started to learn more shit that was
ahead of my self
Then I really start to feel like I couldn't be
around any body else
Other then like minded people
I was cut different

I've always observed people and situations right
in front of me
I think differently
I see the difficulties
I see what human need
I see what people don't see
I see what you don't tell me
I see what you want to be
I see
Differently
After all the shit I seen
I
Still don't judge
It's just apart of my character to see shit the way
that I see as apart of my destiny
That's why people really fuck with me
I realize my spirit no longer wants me to hide
The beauty within me
Is the gift that was given to me
To see the differences between every human
I've allowed others to alter what I seen by
Letting them tell me what I seen
By making me judge-mental with them
But they be judge mental within
Can't mistake that with my super power any
more
Because I know what I'm here for
See half the time these people talking about
other people

Don't really know why they was born
So I realize I had to separate my self
From those because I know my mission
I've been way too distant
For way too long
I am coming back different 💯🖤

Mystery

My motherhood is different from yours
I came here straight from my mothers womb
Got Passed on to another mother near you
I got to a certain age where I realized
Our colors wasn't the same shade
Then I sat down in the court room
Where they tell me who's my new mother and
father the same day
That day was mad sunny
Yet I still felt the shade
They asked me how do I feel
I said great
We celebrated at Wendy's I believe
There was joy in the air
Free from foster care into a home
Where eventually I got to a place where I ain't
care
Something happened where I lost a sense of
freedom
It's when I got older that I realized I lost myself
The freedom to be me or them
Whatever that may be
At the time I remember
Going to school and not comprehending
Certain shit I just pretended

Until my name got called
And I asked them what's the question again
I had a hard time asking for help
Because I'd rather sit and talk shit with myself
Here I am up in the middle of the night
Because my son won't stop crying at night
Fighting for comfort
In a new place called home
Where I sense peace and expansion
I'm just ready to blow
The universe keep telling me
I came here to tell stories
I guess that's why it's been hard for me

This Orgasm was different!

I'm cummin
Like never before
I had an orgasm
That got me pushing through a different door
Now that I'm experiencing this feeling
I want more
Not the kind that makes you moan
But the kind that makes you morn
Grief from letting go of my old self
And everything else
That's keeping me torn
I've finally learned a lesson
Of why self love had to be so hard and
depressing
Because I've come here again learning
The same got damn lesson
To become to the best version
Of which I've been destined

Notes to self

"Typing up your feelings and then discard the
post
Because mental health is telling you that you are
doing the most
Graphing an idea and never executing
Because mental health is asking you how you
going to do it
when you don't know what your doing"

I am worthy of love..

For many years I was seeking something and I
didn't know it was love now that it is right in
front me.
Sometimes I feel I don't know how to respond to
it.
Sometimes I don't know how to stay in tune
with it
I realized that when love is being shown to me it
can feel uncomfortable,
Yet I give it so easily
As much as I was to trying to feel it in my life
Now that I finally feel it from time to time
I have to remind myself
That I am worthy of love

The Blues?

It was the day I came home with Amunet, I came to a home I didn't really feel home in due to conditions and the environment it was in called

 "Kensington" but it was our home for the time being. I remember my girlfriend dropping us off to my house and she stayed while the hubby was in and out the house making moves to provide for the family so he couldn't be home like I wanted him to be. The "blues" happened for me when me and the baby was packing up to stay in our bedroom for the rest of the day, at this point my girlfriend had left so it was just us including the hubby. I went to use the bathroom and quietly slid the door until it clicked securely. The hubby walked to the front of the door and asked me if I was okay? That question set it off. I told him yea I'm okay, he said okay I have to go make a run i'll be back I love you. I said okay. I remember just crying hysterically like someone died or something. I just wasn't okay and I didn't say

I wasn't. I dealt with the pain I was feeling quietly. I stood up even if my stitch hurted. Still I act like I was super fine. I cried because I

didn't know that with physically having the baby
I was going to feel so sad & lonely. I didn't
know that I was going to feel sadness during
these moments of joy. it didn't make
sense to me at the time though I dragged that
feeling with me for so long. then I realized the
doctor warning me of a shift in hormones and
emotions she called it "the blues" that was when
I started to research so much knowledge on the
woman's brain and body before and after having
a baby. that door opened so many doors!!!
I remember learning enough so that I can
explain to my babe about this stuff I was
geeked! at first the approach didn't go so well
because I was too emotional about it and he was
not to opened minded about it at the time due to
his experiences. but with time he learned so
much about woman that he is forever expressing
his gratitude on how much he has learned about
woman and our nature because of me. while he
was learning about woman I learned a lot about
men and their blues!
that's another story to eventually tell...:-)

I am a queen

I am a queen

Growing up I did not hear words as such.
In fact it was probably too much of a high status
for me.
Beautiful may have been the word I was
expecting
But I did not hear that either until I met my king
He has been reminding me how much of a queen
I am ever since
It makes me smile
but deep down I had to work on that belief
therefore I am a queen

I am confident

I had a lot more confidence before becoming a
mother
I became responsible for my self
My daughter, my step daughter, my king on a
daily basis
They had such confidence in me, I lost it by
trying to keep up with the role that is expected
of me
I have hopes and dreams that require confidence
And noticed how pure the confidence is in my
daughters
They want to be just like me
But I don't want them to grow up with lack of
confidence because of my own lack of
confidence
Therefore affirm I am confident

I am a mother

I am a mother
I did not accept my motherhood journey
For a while, I found myself complaining
About it more then I enjoyed it
For a minute I thought I was raising my step
daughter temporarily..
I had to work on accepting being her mother for
the rest of her life and not for the moment
I was focusing more on the problems than the
beauty of it
I realized I had 2 blessings right in front of me
I knew that in the struggle of balancing
motherhood
I wanted to be their mothers, so accepting
motherhood and what comes with It is a must
Therefore I affirm I am a mother

I appreciate money

Because I really hate the fact that money
Had a lot of control of my happiness,
When I don't have it
I am not happy
I start thinking about everything I need
And everything my family need from me
All that I want
All that my family wants
Money if you allow it
It really controls
Your happiness
Stops you from smiling
Makes you cry
a lot

I am mothernurture

I am mothernurture

My best friend and I were sitting on my couch talking about names that I would address myself as and she came up with this one. I changed my name on instagram to mothernurture. I remember going to an event with my best friend and I had a moment about my name because someone asked me "what do you do?" and my best friend answered she is mothernurture! I remember when we left,
I told her how I felt weird about it but in a bad way, it made me realized that I had never really said in public like " hey I'm mothernurture" that night I was asked what do you do it made me think like oh shit I am really mother nurture! Damn I love nature, I love talking about self love, I love teaching people how to heal themselves, I love herbs, plants, positive lectures, aromas, sipping tea and talking about deep shit. I had a realization that I needed to affirm who I am so that I can believe that I am what I love
I am mothernurture by nature

I am living my truths

I found myself not living my truth. I was partially living my truth with myself, with my family, with my adoptive family, with my friends and with social media. I was withholding truth because I was being too considerate of those that wouldn't accept me for me. I was afraid to be vulnerable and get feedback as if my feelings weren't valid. Becoming a mother became tiring quick, therefore I refused to continue to feel tired of not living my truth, and speaking how I feel. It is a working process. Living partially real is a job in itself!

I am fearless

I am fearless

I lived a fearful life. My mother who raised me was a woman who lived in constant fear because her life depended on religion and pleasing god pretty much. Pleasing her pastors and peers at church was more important then pleasing herself or her family. She feared the public, she feared driving to far places, she feared standing up for herself, she feared that she would go to hell for the things I felt was too simple to. She feared alot of shit and therefore when I got into a relationship I found myself and I found a lot of shit I was dealing with. My partner would tell me about myself and I would reflect I couldn't deny my own shit. I realized I am a lot like my mother who raised me and it was effecting me and my family. That's where the choice of affirming "I am fearless" come in..

Self expression is my essence

It is my essence that I speak, I struggle with speaking when is my turn to speak because it is something I wasn't use to. I suppressed what I think and what I know for so long. I am working on coming out my shell to speak what's on my mind, body and soul. I get nervous terrified . The one thing I enjoy doing is sharing wisdom and speaking about self love which Is very sensitive topic for some. I was giving myself that excuse to keep quiet but I have been doing work regarding my throat chakra and affirmations on speaking and I am accepting that self expression is my essence..

Notes to self

" I was too busy trying to fix things about me that the universe said honey those things are unique! so I missed a lot of opportunities in life with doubt, I refuse to lose now"